how2become.com

Army Aptitude Tests: Spatial Reasoning & Rule Analysis

Practice Tests for the British Army
Assessment Centre

www.How2Become.com

As part of this product you have also received **FREE** access to online tests that will help you to pass the Army Aptitude Tests:

To gain access, simply go to:

www.MyPsychometricTests.co.uk

Get more products for passing any test at:

www.How2Become.com

Orders: Please contact How2Become Ltd, Suite 1, 60 Churchill Square Business Centre, Kings Hill, Kent ME19 4YU.

You can order through Amazon.co.uk under ISBN: 9781912370689, via the website www.How2Become.com or through Gardners.com.

ISBN: 9781912370689

First published in 2019 by How2Become Ltd.

Copyright © 2019 How2Become.

Front cover image has been used under the Open Government Licence 3.0

Typeset by Gemma Butler for How2Become Ltd.

Disclaimer

Every effort has been made to ensure that the information contained within this guide is accurate at the time of publication. How2Become Ltd is not responsible for anyone failing any part of any selection process as a result of the information contained within this guide. How2Become Ltd and their authors cannot accept any responsibility for any errors or omissions within this guide, however caused. No responsibility for loss or damage occasioned by any person acting, or refraining from action, as a result of the material in this publication can be accepted by How2Become Ltd.

The information within this guide does not represent the views of any third party service or organisation.

CONTENTS

Introduction

Welcome to *Army Aptitude Tests: Spatial Reasoning & Rule Analysis*. This guide contains lots of sample test questions that are appropriate for anyone who is applying to join the British Army.

The selection test for the army is designed to assess potential Armed Forces personnel's 'suitability' for specific posts. The higher scores you achieve, the more job opportunities you will have at your disposal. Whilst the minimum pass mark for entry into the army is 26, a candidate will need to score far higher if he or she wishes to join a regiment such as the Royal Electrical and Mechanical Engineers.

The key to success is to try your hardest to get 100% correct answers in the test that you are undertaking. If you aim for 100% in your preparation, then you are far more likely to achieve the trade or career that you want.

We have supplied you with lots of sample questions to assist you. It is crucial that when you get a question wrong, you take the time to find out why you got it wrong.

Understanding the question is very important. You will find that the more practice you undertake in the build up to the real test, the better you will perform on the day.

Please note that the tests in this book are not an exact replication of those that you will sit as part of the Army Aptitude Tests. These tests are designed to assess the same skills that you will need in order to pass the real Army Aptitude Tests. So, while these tests may differ from those that you will face in the exam, improving your abilities in these tests will still prepare you for the Army Aptitude Tests.

In addition to the tests within this guide we would also like to give you free access to our online psychometric testing facility.

To gain access to our suite, simply go to the following website:

www.PsychometricTestsOnline.co.uk

Good luck and best wishes,

The how2become team

The How2Become Team

Spatial Reasoning

For the following test, you will need to memorise two rules, then visualise applying them to two shapes.

In each question, you will be provided with two shapes. Each shape will be associated with a rule:

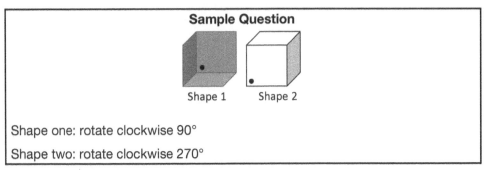

Sample Question

Shape 1 Shape 2

Shape one: rotate clockwise 90°

Shape two: rotate clockwise 270°

You have 10 seconds to memorise these shapes, as well as their two associated rules. Once the 10 seconds expire, you will have to recall the rules and the positions of the shapes to find the correct answer.

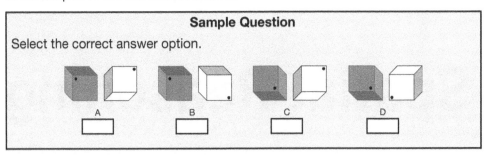

Sample Question

Select the correct answer option.

A   B   C   D

To answer this question, you need to apply the rules, visualising them in your head. To make this easier, figure out one shape at a time.

Starting with Shape 1, rotate the shape clockwise by 90°.

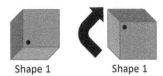

Shape 1   Shape 1

This gives us the answer for shape one, eliminating answer options C and D since they don't match. With only answer options A and B remaining, we can move onto Shape 2, which must be rotated clockwise by 270°:

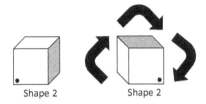

Shape 2   Shape 2

This gives us the answer for Shape 2.

With these two new shapes, we can identify the correct answer option: B.

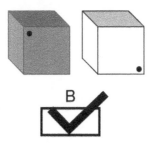

TEST 1 WILL BEGIN ON THE NEXT PAGE

Spatial Reasoning – Test 1

Answer one question at a time. Memorise the two shapes, and the rule for each shape. You have 30 seconds to memorise these before turning the page to answer the questions.

Question 1.

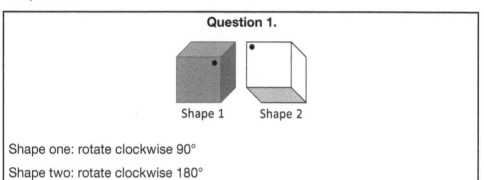

Shape 1   Shape 2

Shape one: rotate clockwise 90°

Shape two: rotate clockwise 180°

Question 2.

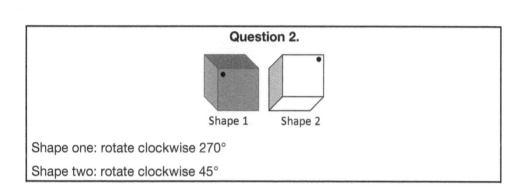

Shape 1   Shape 2

Shape one: rotate clockwise 270°

Shape two: rotate clockwise 45°

Question 3.

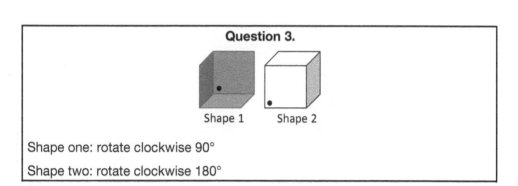

Shape 1   Shape 2

Shape one: rotate clockwise 90°

Shape two: rotate clockwise 180°

Question 1.

Select the correct answer option.

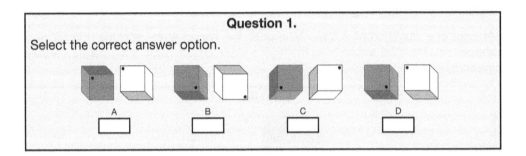

A

B

C

D

Question 2.

Select the correct answer option.

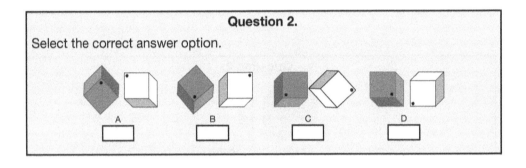

A

B

C

D

Question 3.

Select the correct answer option.

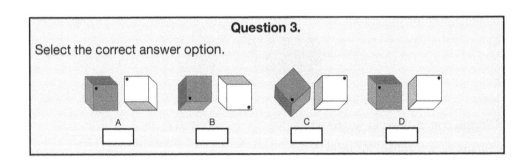

A

B

C

D

Question 4.

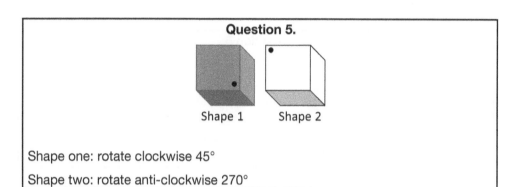

Shape 1   Shape 2

Shape one: rotate clockwise 180°

Shape two: rotate clockwise 360°

Question 5.

Shape 1   Shape 2

Shape one: rotate clockwise 45°

Shape two: rotate anti-clockwise 270°

Question 6.

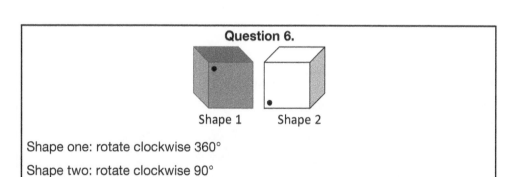

Shape 1   Shape 2

Shape one: rotate clockwise 360°

Shape two: rotate clockwise 90°

Question 4.

Select the correct answer option.

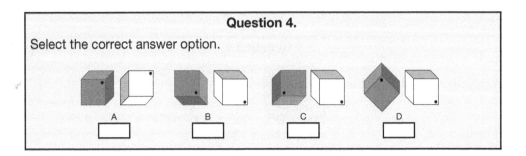

A B C D

Question 5.

Select the correct answer option.

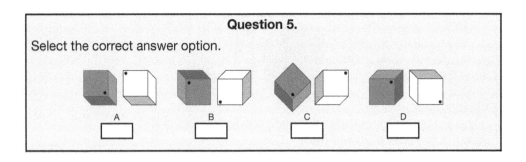

A B C D

Question 6.

Select the correct answer option.

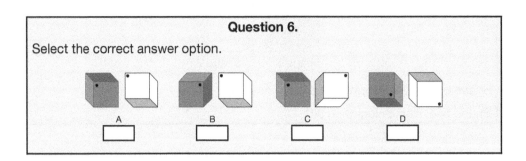

A B C D

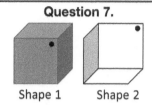

Question 7.

Shape 1   Shape 2

Shape one: rotate clockwise 135°

Shape two: rotate clockwise 90°

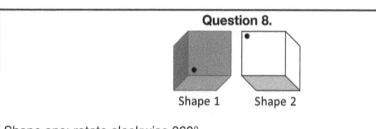

Question 8.

Shape 1   Shape 2

Shape one: rotate clockwise 360°

Shape two: rotate anti-clockwise 180°

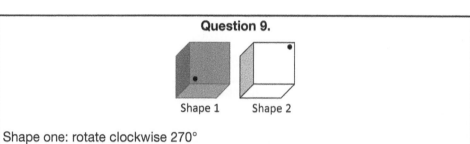

Question 9.

Shape 1   Shape 2

Shape one: rotate clockwise 270°

Shape two: rotate clockwise 180°

Question 7.

Select the correct answer option.

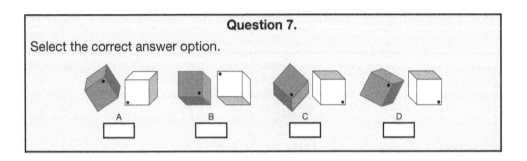

A

B

C

D

Question 8.

Select the correct answer option.

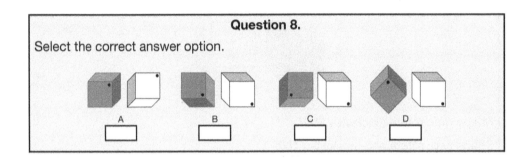

A

B

C

D

Question 9.

Select the correct answer option.

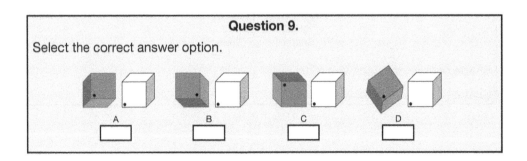

A

B

C

D

Question 10.

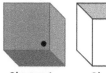

Shape 1   Shape 2

Shape one: rotate clockwise 180°

Shape two: rotate clockwise 45°

Question 11.

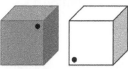

Shape 1   Shape 2

Shape one: rotate clockwise 90°

Shape two: rotate clockwise 315°

Question 12.

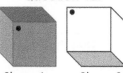

Shape 1   Shape 2

Shape one: rotate clockwise 180°

Shape two: rotate clockwise 45°

Question 10.

Select the correct answer option.

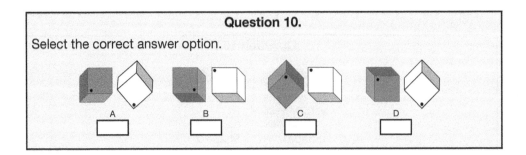

A B C D

Question 11.

Select the correct answer option.

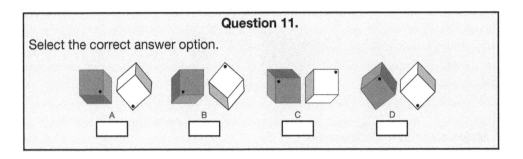

A B C D

Question 12.

Select the correct answer option.

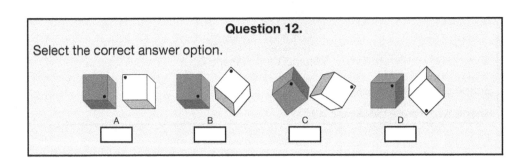

A B C D

Question 13.

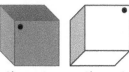

Shape 1   Shape 2

Shape one: rotate clockwise 90°

Shape two: rotate clockwise 90°

Question 14.

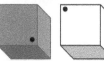

Shape 1   Shape 2

Shape one: rotate clockwise 360°

Shape two: rotate clockwise 270°

Question 15.

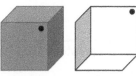

Shape 1   Shape 2

Shape one: rotate clockwise 90°

Shape two: rotate clockwise 135°

Question 13.

Select the correct answer option.

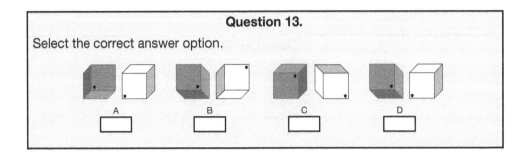

A

B

C

D

Question 14.

Select the correct answer option.

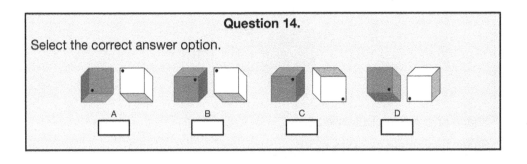

A

B

C

D

Question 15.

Select the correct answer option.

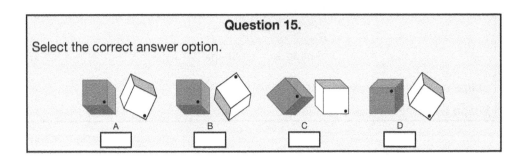

A

B

C

D

ANSWERS OVERLEAF

Q1. B

Q2. C

Q3. D

Q4. C

Q5. C

Q6. A

Q7. C

Q8. C

Q9. B

Q10. D

Q11. A

Q12. B

Q13. C

Q14. D

Q15. A

Spatial Reasoning – Test 2

Answer one question at a time. Memorise the two shapes, and the rule for each shape. You have 30 seconds to memorise these before turning the page to answer the questions.

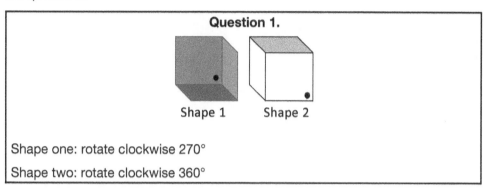

Question 1.

Shape 1   Shape 2

Shape one: rotate clockwise 270°

Shape two: rotate clockwise 360°

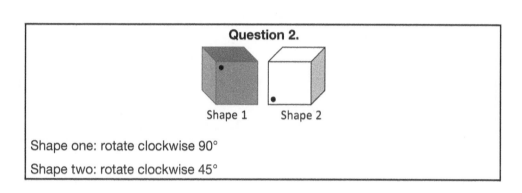

Question 2.

Shape 1   Shape 2

Shape one: rotate clockwise 90°

Shape two: rotate clockwise 45°

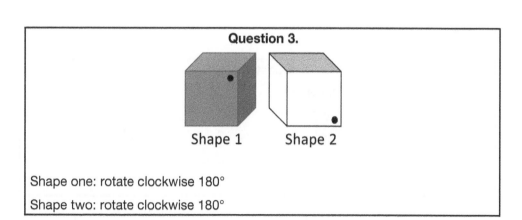

Question 3.

Shape 1   Shape 2

Shape one: rotate clockwise 180°

Shape two: rotate clockwise 180°

Question 1.

Select the correct answer option.

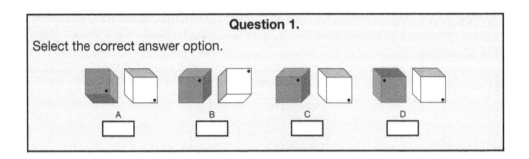

A	B	C	D

Question 2.

Select the correct answer option.

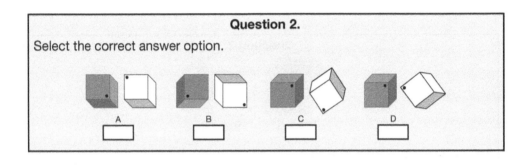

A	B	C	D

Question 3.

Select the correct answer option.

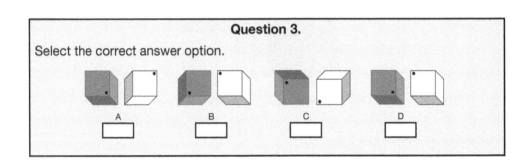

A	B	C	D

Question 4.

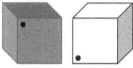

Shape 1   Shape 2

Shape one: rotate clockwise 270°

Shape two: rotate anti-clockwise 45°

Question 5.

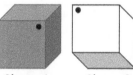

Shape 1   Shape 2

Shape one: rotate anti-clockwise 45°

Shape two: rotate clockwise 180°

Question 6.

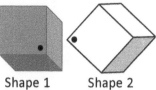

Shape 1   Shape 2

Shape one: rotate clockwise 90°

Shape two: rotate anti-clockwise 90°

Question 4.

Select the correct answer option.

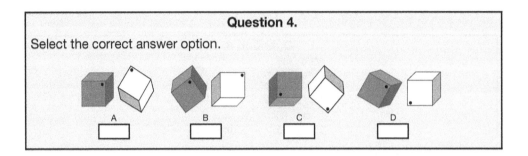

A	B	C	D

Question 5.

Select the correct answer option.

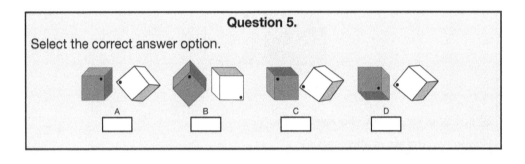

A	B	C	D

Question 6.

Select the correct answer option.

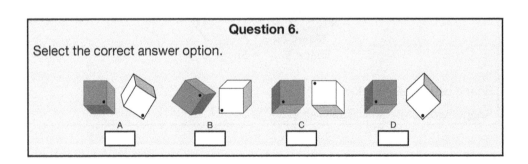

A	B	C	D

Question 7.

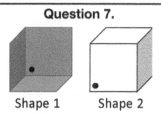

Shape 1   Shape 2

Shape one: rotate clockwise 135°

Shape two: rotate anti-clockwise 45°

Question 8.

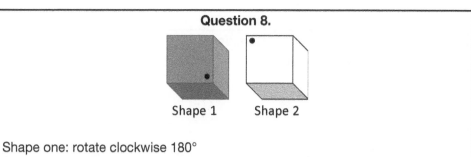

Shape 1   Shape 2

Shape one: rotate clockwise 180°

Shape two: rotate clockwise 270°

Question 9.

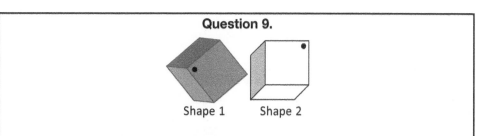

Shape 1   Shape 2

Shape one: rotate anti-clockwise 45°

Shape two: rotate anti-clockwise 90°

Question 7.

Select the correct answer option.

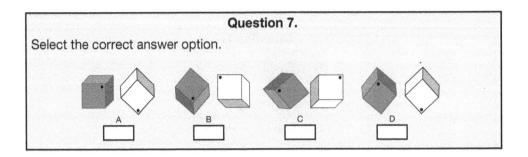

A B C D

Question 8.

Select the correct answer option.

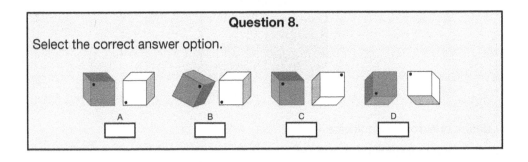

A B C D

Question 9.

Select the correct answer option.

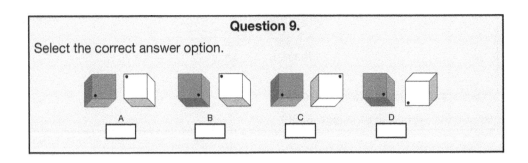

A B C D

Question 10.

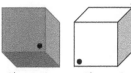

Shape 1   Shape 2

Shape one: rotate anti-clockwise 270°

Shape two: rotate clockwise 90°

Question 11.

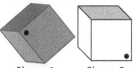

Shape 1   Shape 2

Shape one: rotate anti-clockwise 135°

Shape two: rotate anti-clockwise 90°

Question 12.

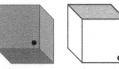

Shape 1   Shape 2

Shape one: rotate clockwise 90°

Shape two: rotate anti-clockwise 45°

Question 10.

Select the correct answer option.

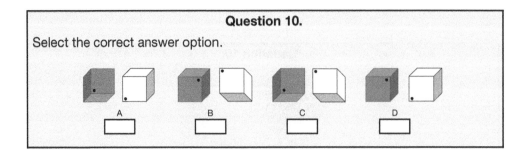

A ☐   B ☐   C ☐   D ☐

Question 11.

Select the correct answer option.

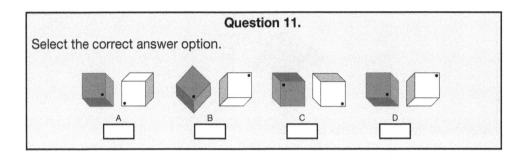

A ☐   B ☐   C ☐   D ☐

Question 12.

Select the correct answer option.

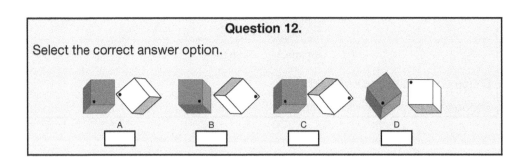

A ☐   B ☐   C ☐   D ☐

Question 13.

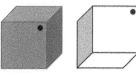

Shape 1   Shape 2

Shape one: rotate clockwise 45°

Shape two: rotate clockwise 315°

Question 14.

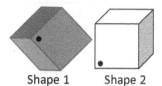

Shape 1   Shape 2

Shape one: rotate anti-clockwise 45°

Shape two: rotate anti-clockwise 405°

Question 15.

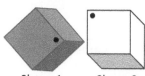

Shape 1   Shape 2

Shape one: rotate clockwise 180°

Shape two: rotate anti-clockwise 270°

Question 13.

Select the correct answer option.

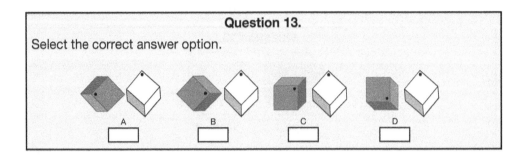

A ☐   B ☐   C ☐   D ☐

Question 14.

Select the correct answer option.

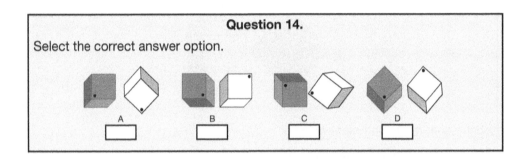

A ☐   B ☐   C ☐   D ☐

Question 15.

Select the correct answer option.

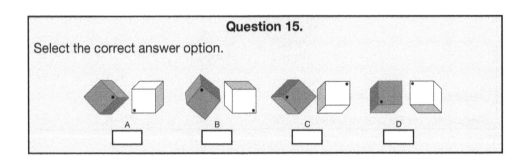

A ☐   B ☐   C ☐   D ☐

ANSWERS OVERLEAF

Q1. C

Q2. D

Q3. B

Q4. C

Q5. B

Q6. D

Q7. D

Q8. A

Q9. A

Q10. C

Q11. D

Q12. C

Q13. B

Q14. A

Q15. C

Spatial Reasoning – Test 3

Answer one question at a time. Memorise the two shapes, and the rule for each shape. You have 30 seconds to memorise these before turning the page to answer the questions.

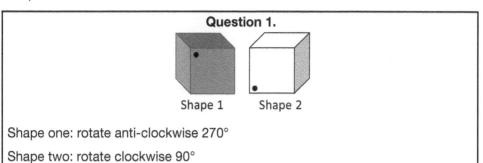

Question 1.

Shape 1   Shape 2

Shape one: rotate anti-clockwise 270°

Shape two: rotate clockwise 90°

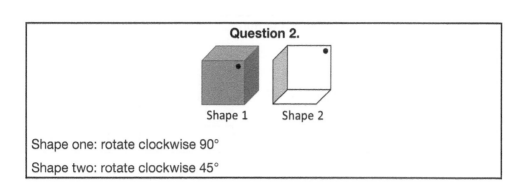

Question 2.

Shape 1   Shape 2

Shape one: rotate clockwise 90°

Shape two: rotate clockwise 45°

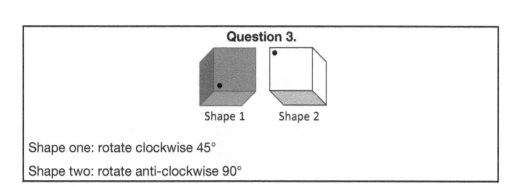

Question 3.

Shape 1   Shape 2

Shape one: rotate clockwise 45°

Shape two: rotate anti-clockwise 90°

Question 1.

Select the correct answer option.

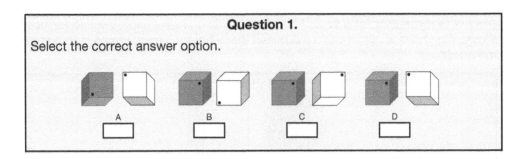

A

B

C

D

Question 2.

Select the correct answer option.

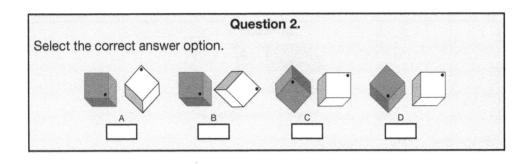

A

B

C

D

Question 3.

Select the correct answer option.

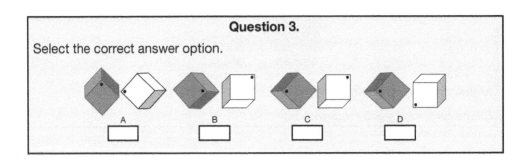

A

B

C

D

Question 4.

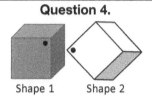

Shape 1   Shape 2

Shape one: rotate anti-clockwise 315°

Shape two: rotate clockwise 45°

Question 5.

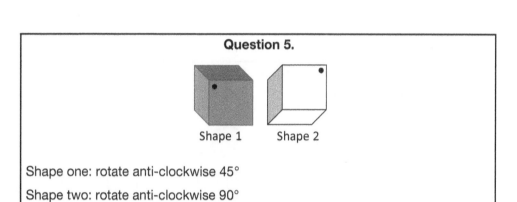

Shape 1   Shape 2

Shape one: rotate anti-clockwise 45°

Shape two: rotate anti-clockwise 90°

Question 6.

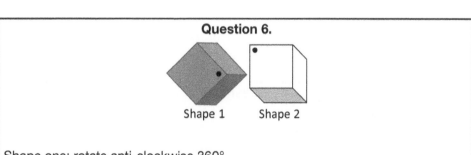

Shape 1   Shape 2

Shape one: rotate anti-clockwise 360°

Shape two: rotate clockwise 45°

Question 4.

Select the correct answer option.

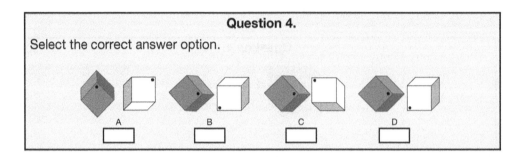

A	B	C	D

Question 5.

Select the correct answer option.

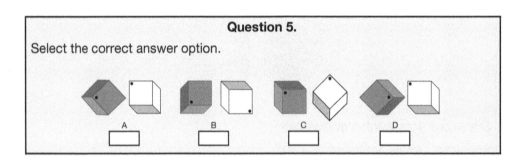

A	B	C	D

Question 6.

Select the correct answer option.

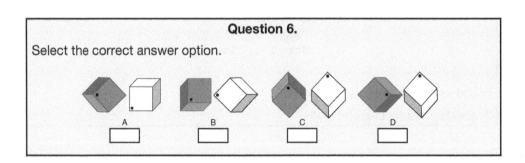

A	B	C	D

Question 7.

Shape 1   Shape 2

Shape one: rotate anti-clockwise 45°

Shape two: rotate clockwise 225°

Question 8.

Shape 1   Shape 2

Shape one: rotate anti-clockwise 90°

Shape two: rotate clockwise 90°

Question 9.

Shape 1   Shape 2

Shape one: rotate anti-clockwise 45°

Shape two: rotate anti-clockwise 135°

Question 7.

Select the correct answer option.

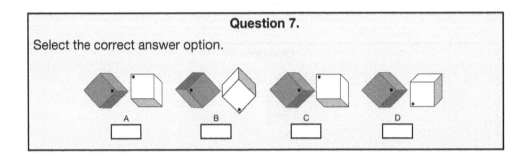

A	B	C	D

Question 8.

Select the correct answer option.

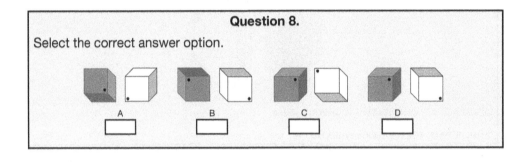

A	B	C	D

Question 9.

Select the correct answer option.

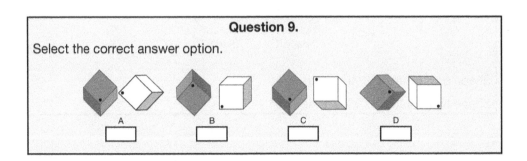

A	B	C	D

Question 10.

Shape 1   Shape 2

Shape one: rotate clockwise 90°

Shape two: rotate anti-clockwise 270°

Question 11.

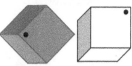

Shape 1   Shape 2

Shape one: rotate clockwise 45°

Shape two: rotate anti-clockwise 45°

Question 12.

Shape 1   Shape 2

Shape one: rotate anti-clockwise 180°

Shape two: rotate clockwise 90°

Question 10.

Select the correct answer option.

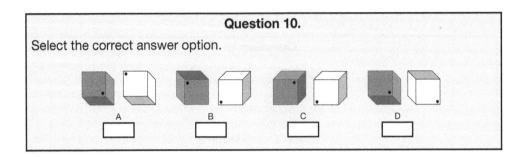

A

B

C

D

Question 11.

Select the correct answer option.

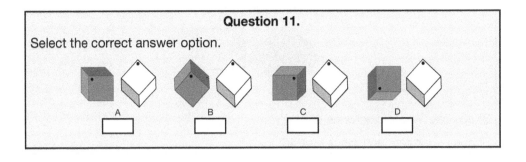

A

B

C

D

Question 12.

Select the correct answer option.

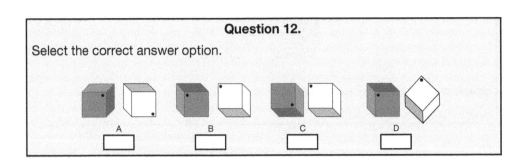

A

B

C

D

Question 13.

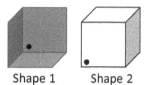

Shape 1   Shape 2

Shape one: rotate anti-clockwise 90°

Shape two: rotate clockwise 270°

Question 14.

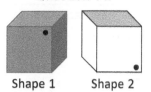

Shape 1   Shape 2

Shape one: rotate clockwise 135°

Shape two: rotate clockwise 45°

Question 15.

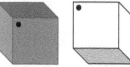

Shape 1   Shape 2

Shape one: rotate anti-clockwise 360°

Shape two: rotate clockwise 45°

Question 13.

Select the correct answer option.

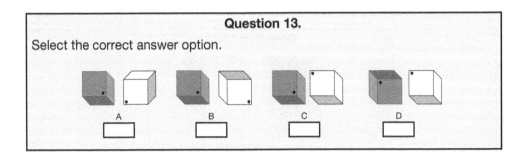

A

B

C

D

Question 14.

Select the correct answer option.

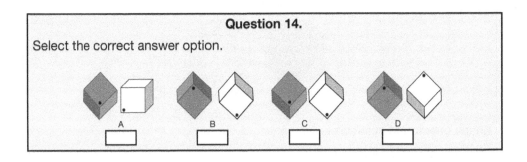

A

B

C

D

Question 15.

Select the correct answer option.

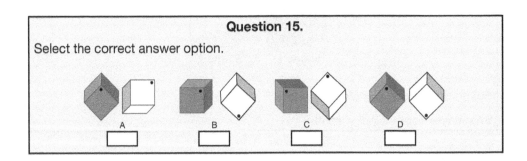

A

B

C

D

ANSWERS OVERLEAF

Q1. D

Q2. B

Q3. D

Q4. C

Q5. A

Q6. D

Q7. B

Q8. D

Q9. A

Q10. C

Q11. A

Q12. A

Q13. B

Q14. C

Q15. C

Spatial Reasoning – Test 4

Answer one question at a time. Memorise the two shapes, and the rule for each shape. You have 30 seconds to memorise these before turning the page to answer the questions.

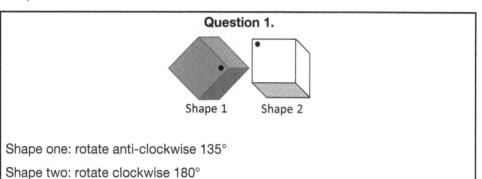

Question 1.

Shape 1   Shape 2

Shape one: rotate anti-clockwise 135°

Shape two: rotate clockwise 180°

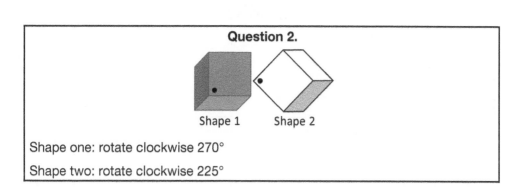

Question 2.

Shape 1   Shape 2

Shape one: rotate clockwise 270°

Shape two: rotate clockwise 225°

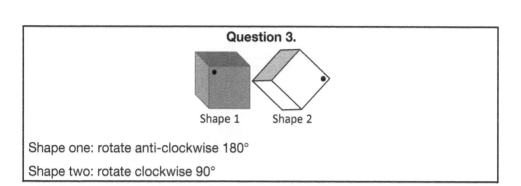

Question 3.

Shape 1   Shape 2

Shape one: rotate anti-clockwise 180°

Shape two: rotate clockwise 90°

Question 1.

Select the correct answer option.

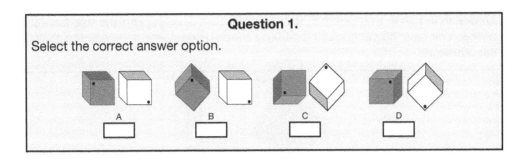

Question 2.

Select the correct answer option.

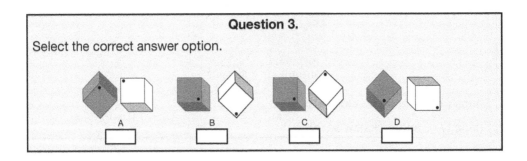

Question 3.

Select the correct answer option.

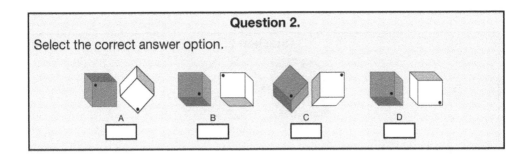

Question 4.

Shape 1   Shape 2

Shape one: rotate anti-clockwise 180°

Shape two: rotate clockwise 180°

Question 5.

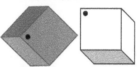

Shape 1   Shape 2

Shape one: rotate clockwise 270°

Shape two: rotate clockwise 90°

Question 6.

Shape 1   Shape 2

Shape one: rotate anti-clockwise 90°

Shape two: rotate clockwise 45°

Question 4.

Select the correct answer option.

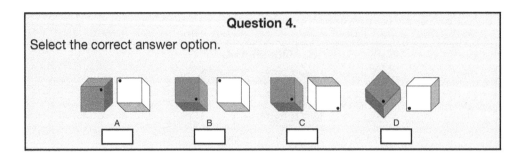

A	B	C	D

Question 5.

Select the correct answer option.

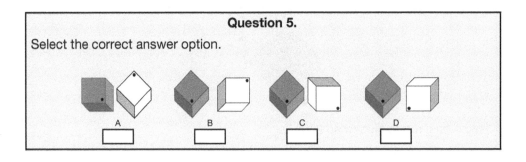

A	B	C	D

Question 6.

Select the correct answer option.

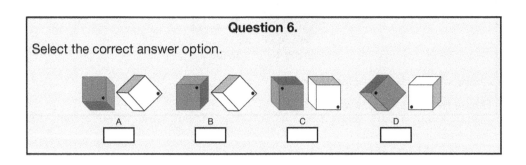

A	B	C	D

Question 7.

Shape 1   Shape 2

Shape one: rotate anti-clockwise 270°

Shape two: rotate clockwise 135°

Question 8.

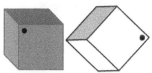

Shape 1   Shape 2

Shape one: rotate anti-clockwise 45°

Shape two: rotate clockwise 180°

Question 9.

Shape 1   Shape 2

Shape one: rotate anti-clockwise 315°

Shape two: rotate clockwise 135°

Question 7.

Select the correct answer option.

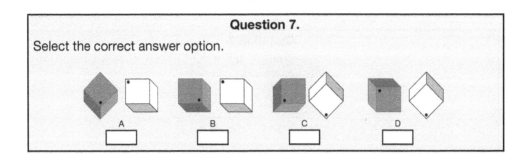

A	B	C	D

Question 8.

Select the correct answer option.

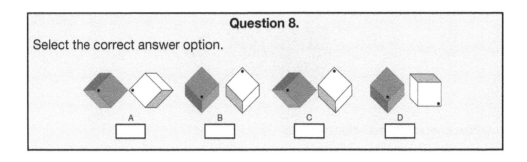

A	B	C	D

Question 9.

Select the correct answer option.

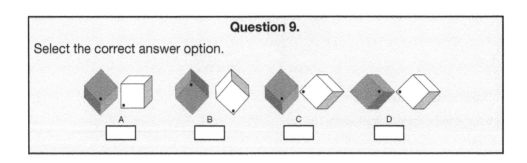

A	B	C	D

Question 10.

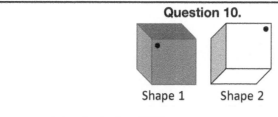

Shape 1   Shape 2

Shape one: rotate clockwise 135°

Shape two: rotate clockwise 135°

Question 11.

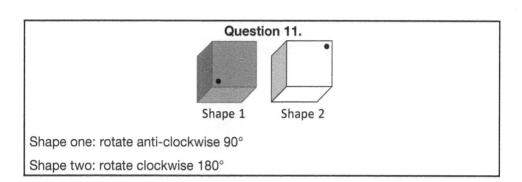

Shape 1   Shape 2

Shape one: rotate anti-clockwise 90°

Shape two: rotate clockwise 180°

Question 12.

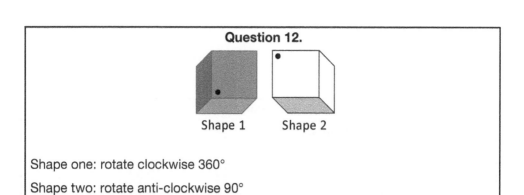

Shape 1   Shape 2

Shape one: rotate clockwise 360°

Shape two: rotate anti-clockwise 90°

Question 10.

Select the correct answer option.

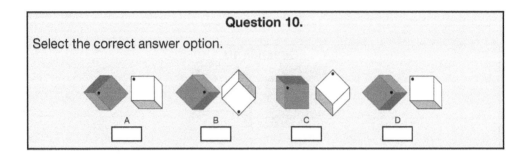

A

B

C

D

Question 11.

Select the correct answer option.

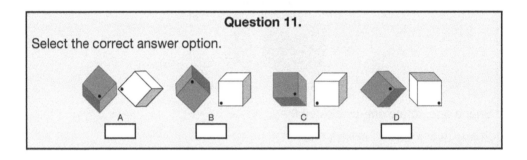

A

B

C

D

Question 12.

Select the correct answer option.

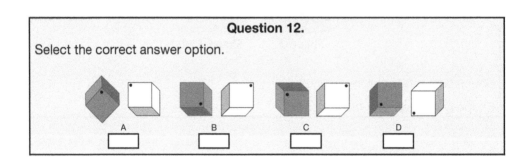

A

B

C

D

Question 13.

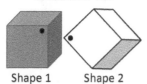

Shape 1   Shape 2

Shape one: rotate clockwise 90°

Shape two: rotate clockwise 45°

Question 14.

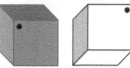

Shape 1   Shape 2

Shape one: rotate clockwise 90°

Shape two: rotate anti-clockwise 270°

Question 15.

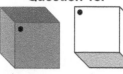

Shape 1   Shape 2

Shape one: rotate clockwise 90°

Shape two: rotate clockwise 180°

Question 13.

Select the correct answer option.

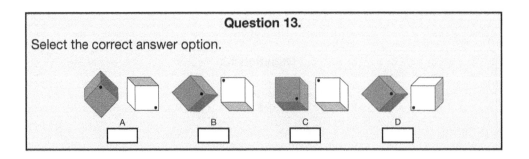

A
B
C
D

Question 14.

Select the correct answer option.

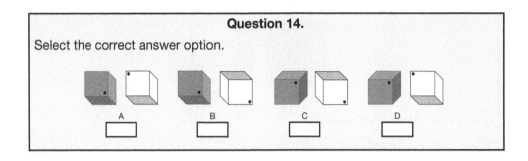

A
B
C
D

Question 15.

Select the correct answer option.

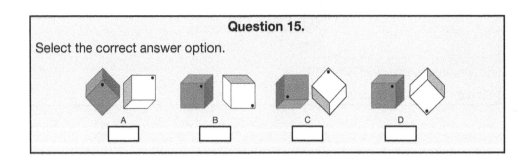

A
B
C
D

ANSWERS OVERLEAF

Q1. A

Q2. D

Q3. B

Q4. A

Q5. B

Q6. B

Q7. D

Q8. A

Q9. D

Q10. B

Q11. C

Q12. D

Q13. C

Q14. C

Q15. B

Rule Analysis

For the following test, memorise the symbols as per the direction of the arrows and choose the correct answer from the options below.

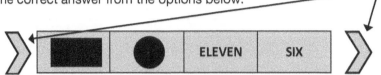

The above sequence is telling you to memorise from left to right. You will have 20 seconds per question. Once the 20 seconds are up, turn over the page and you will be presented with three answer options. Each answer option will contain a list of rules. You must select the option which contains the four rules that apply to the sequence.

Circle Precedes Square	Shapes Precede Two-Digit Number	Even Follows Odd
Shapes Precede Two-Digit Number	Even Precedes Odd	Circle Follows Rectangle
Numbers Follow Rectangle	Circle Precedes Rectangle	Rectangle Precedes Even
Even Follows Odd	Numbers Follow Rectangle	Circle Precedes Even

There may be rules in the answer options that are not relevant to the sequence you have memorised. For example, the first rule in option 1 is 'Circle Precedes Square'. As there are no squares in the sequence, this rule is not applicable, so you can discount answer option 1.

Based on the sequence the only matching choice is the right-hand choice. The even number follows the odd number (six is after eleven), circle follows rectangle. The rectangle precedes the even number and the circle precedes the even number.

Reversed arrows

Pay close attention to the direction in which the outside arrows are pointing. With this variation of the test you will need to read the symbols from right to left. So, the sequence is four, thirteen, circle, and triangle.

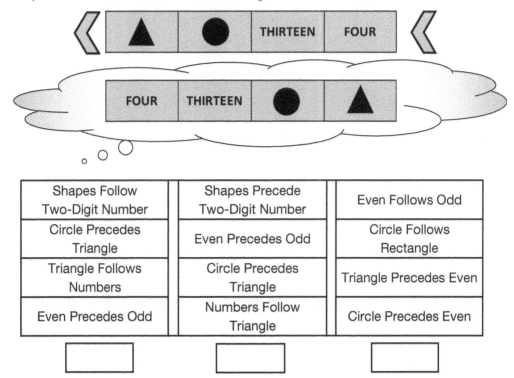

Shapes Follow Two-Digit Number	Shapes Precede Two-Digit Number	Even Follows Odd
Circle Precedes Triangle	Even Precedes Odd	Circle Follows Rectangle
Triangle Follows Numbers	Circle Precedes Triangle	Triangle Precedes Even
Even Precedes Odd	Numbers Follow Triangle	Circle Precedes Even

Based on the above sequence, the only matching choice is the left hand choice, shapes follow the two-digit number, circle precedes triangle, triangle follows numbers, even precedes odd.

TEST 1 WILL BEGIN ON THE NEXT PAGE

Rule Analysis – Test 1

You have 20 seconds to memorise the order of the list as per the direction of the arrows. Then turn over the page and identify the rules which match the order below.

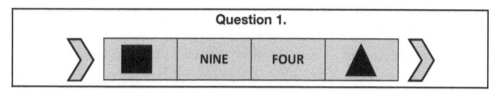

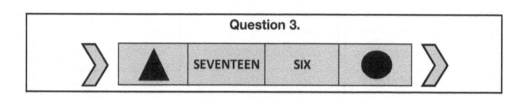

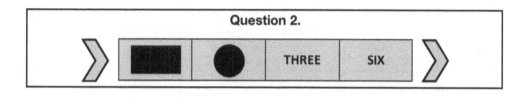

Question 1.

Even Follows Odd	Even Precedes Odd	Even Precedes Odd
Square Precedes Numbers	Shapes Precede Numbers	Shapes Precede Numbers
Triangle Follows Odd	Square Precedes Circle	Square Precedes Circle
Nine Follows Square	Two Digits Follow Single Digits	Two Digits Follow Single Digits

Question 2.

Shapes Precede Numbers	Circle Follows Square	Odd Precedes Even
Rectangle Precedes Circle	Odd Follows Even	Shapes Precede Numbers
Two Digits Follow Single Digits	Two Digits Precede Single Digits	Odd Follows Circle
Even Precedes Odd	Square Follows Numbers	Circle Follows Rectangle

Question 3.

Triangle Precedes Numbers	Circle Follows Numbers	Circle Follows Triangle
Circle Follows Triangle	Triangle Precedes Numbers	Triangle Follows Numbers
Numbers Follow Circle	Odd Precedes Even	Odd Precedes Even
Two Digits Precede Single Digits	Numbers Precede Circle	Numbers Precede Circle

Question 4.

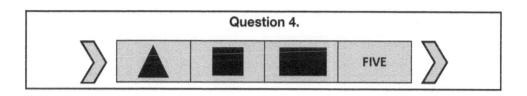

Question 5.

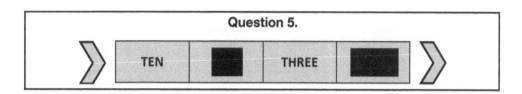

Question 6.

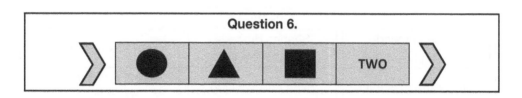

Question 4.

Square Precedes Number	Rectangle Follows Square	Circle Follows Triangle
Triangle Follows Square	Square Precedes Number	Rectangle Precedes Circle
Number Precedes Circle	Rectangle Follows Triangle	Square Follows Triangle
Circle Follows Triangle	Number Follows Square	Triangle Precedes Square

Question 5.

Triangle Precedes Single-Digit Number	Rectangle Follows Numbers	Even Precedes Odd
Triangle Follows Rectangle	Odd Follows Even	Triangle Follows Two-Digit Number
Rectangle Follows Numbers	Even Precedes Square	Rectangle Precedes Triangle
Even Follows Odd	Rectangle Follows Square	Rectangle Follows Numbers

Question 6.

Shapes Precede One-Digit Number	Shapes Precede Number	Even Precedes Odd
Circle Precedes Even	Even Follows Odd	Circle Precedes Rectangle
Number Follows Square	Circle Precedes Rectangle	Rectangle Precedes Even
Square Follows Circle	Even Follows Shapes	Circle Follows Even

Question 7.

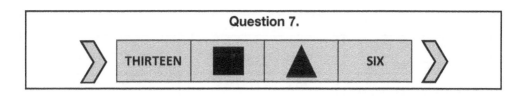

Question 8.

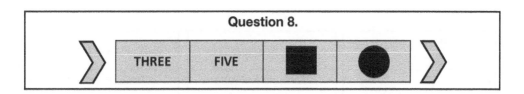

Question 9.

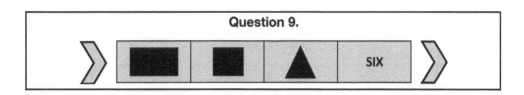

Question 7.

Shapes Precede One-Digit Number	Shapes Precede Even	Even Precedes Odd
Circle Precedes Even	Triangle Follows Square	Circle Precedes Rectangle
Numbers Follow Square	Square Precedes Triangle	Rectangle Precedes Even
Square Follows Circle	Odd Precedes Shapes	Circle Follows Even

Question 8.

Shapes Follow One-Digit Numbers	Shapes Precede Even	Even Precedes Odd
Circle Follows Odd	Triangle Follows Square	Circle Precedes Rectangle
Square Follows Numbers	Square Precedes Triangle	Rectangle Precedes Even
Square Precedes Circle	Odd Precedes Shapes	Circle Follows Even

Question 9.

Shapes Precede One-Digit Number	Shapes Precede Even	Triangle Precedes Even
Circle Precedes Even	Triangle Follows Square	Rectangle Precedes Square
Number Follows Square	Square Precedes Triangle	Rectangle Precedes Even
Square Follows Circle	Odd Precedes Shapes	Square Follows Rectangle

Question 10.

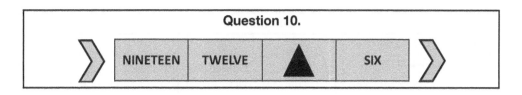

Question 11.

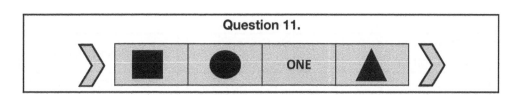

Question 12.

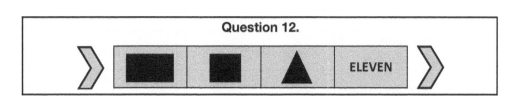

Question 10.

Shape Precedes One Digit Number	Shape Precedes Even	Even Precedes Odd
Triangle Precedes Even One-Number Digit	Triangle Follows Square	Circle Precedes Rectangle
One Digit Follows Triangle	Square Precedes Triangle	Rectangle Precedes Even
Triangle Follows Odd	Odd Precedes Shapes	Circle Follows Even

Question 11.

Shapes Precede One-Digit Number	Circle Precedes Number	Even Precedes Odd
Circle Precedes Even	Triangle Follows Circle	Circle Precedes Rectangle
Number Follows Square	Square Precedes Triangle	Rectangle Precedes Even
Square Follows Circle	Square Precedes Number	Circle Follows Even

Question 12.

Shapes Precede One-Digit Number	Shapes Precede Odd	Even Precedes Odd
Circle Precedes Even	Triangle Follows Square	Circle Precedes Rectangle
Number Follows Square	Square Precedes Triangle	Rectangle Precedes Even
Square Follows Circle	Odd Follows Shapes	Circle Follows Even

Question 13.

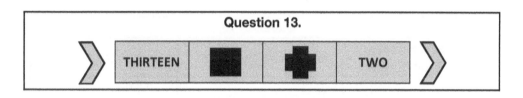

Question 14.

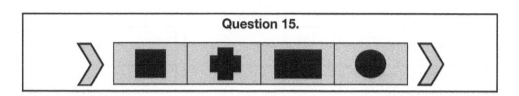

Question 15.

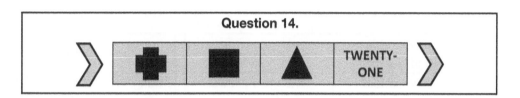

Question 13.

Shapes Precede One-Digit Number	Shapes Precede Even	Even Precedes Odd
Even Follows Cross	Triangle Follows Cross	Circle Precedes Rectangle
Cross Follows Square	Circle Precedes Even	Rectangle Precedes Even
Square Follows Odd	Odd Precedes Shapes	Circle Precedes Even

Question 14.

Shapes Precede Two-Digit Number	Shapes Precede Even	Even Precedes Odd
Cross Precedes Triangle	Triangle Follows Square	Triangle Precedes Even One-Number Digit
Odd Follows Square	Square Precedes Triangle	Rectangle Precedes Even
Square Follows Cross	Shapes Follow Odd	Circle Follows Even

Question 15.

Square Precedes Circle	Shapes Precede Even	Even Precedes Odd
Cross Precedes Rectangle	Triangle Follows Square	Circle Follows Rectangle
Circle Follows Square	Square Precedes Triangle	Cross Follows Square
Square Precedes Cross	Two Digits Follow Single Digits	Square Precedes Circle

ANSWERS OVERLEAF

Question 1.

Even Follows Odd	Even Precedes Odd	Even Precedes Odd
Square Precedes Numbers	Shapes Precede Numbers	Shapes Precede Numbers
Triangle Follows Odd	Square Precedes Circle	Square Precedes Circle
Nine Follows Square	Two Digits Follow Single Digits	Two Digits Follow Single Digits
✓		

Question 2.

Shapes Precede Numbers	Circle Follows Square	Odd Precedes Even
Rectangle Precedes Circle	Odd Follows Even	Shapes Precede Numbers
Two Digits Follow Single Digits	Two Digits Precede Single Digits	Odd Follows Circle
Even Precedes Odd	Square Follows Numbers	Circle Follows Rectangle
		✓

Question 3.

Triangle Precedes Numbers	Circle Follows Numbers	Circle Follows Triangle
Circle Follows Triangle	Triangle Precedes Numbers	Triangle Follows Numbers
Numbers Follow Circle	Odd Precedes Even	Odd Precedes Even
Two Digits Precede Single Digits	Numbers Precede Circle	Numbers Precede Circle
	✓	

Question 4.

Square Precedes Number	Rectangle Follows Square	Circle Follows Triangle
Triangle Follows Square	Square Precedes Number	Rectangle Precedes Circle
Number Precedes Circle	Rectangle Follows Triangle	Square Follows Triangle
Circle Follows Triangle	Number Follows Square	Triangle Precedes Square
	✓	

Question 5.

Triangle Precedes Single-Digit Number	Rectangle Follows Numbers	Even Precedes Odd
Triangle Follows Rectangle	Odd Follows Even	Triangle Follows Two-Digit Number
Rectangle Follows Numbers	Even Precedes Square	Rectangle Precedes Triangle
Even Follows Odd	Rectangle Follows Square	Rectangle Follows Numbers
	✓	

Question 6.

Shapes Precede One-Digit Number	Shapes Precede Number	Even Precedes Odd
Circle Precedes Even	Even Follows Odd	Circle Precedes Rectangle
Number Follows Square	Circle Precedes Rectangle	Rectangle Precedes Even
Square Follows Circle	Even Follows Shapes	Circle Follows Even
✓		

Question 7.

Shapes Precede One-Digit Number	Shapes Precede Even	Even Precedes Odd
Circle Precedes Even	Triangle Follows Square	Circle Precedes Rectangle
Numbers Follow Square	Square Precedes Triangle	Rectangle Precedes Even
Square Follows Circle	Odd Precedes Shapes	Circle Follows Even
☐	✓	☐

Question 8.

Shapes Follow One-Digit Numbers	Shapes Precede Even	Even Precedes Odd
Circle Follows Odd	Triangle Follows Square	Circle Precedes Rectangle
Square Follows Numbers	Square Precedes Triangle	Rectangle Precedes Even
Square Precedes Circle	Odd Precedes Shapes	Circle Follows Even
✓	☐	☐

Question 9.

Shapes Precede One-Digit Number	Shapes Precede Even	Triangle Precedes Even
Circle Precedes Even	Triangle Follows Square	Rectangle Precedes Square
Number Follows Square	Square Precedes Triangle	Rectangle Precedes Even
Square Follows Circle	Odd Precedes Shapes	Square Follows Rectangle
☐	☐	✓

Question 10.		
Shape Precedes One Digit Number	Shapes Precede Even	Even Precedes Odd
Triangle Precedes Even One-Number Digit	Triangle Follows Square	Circle Precedes Rectangle
One Digit Follows Triangle	Square Precedes Triangle	Rectangle Precedes Even
Triangle Follows Odd	Odd Precedes Shapes	Circle Follows Even
✓		

Question 11.		
Shapes Precede One-Digit Number	Circle Precedes Number	Even Precedes Odd
Circle Precedes Even	Triangle Follows Circle	Circle Precedes Rectangle
Numbers Follow Square	Square Precedes Triangle	Rectangle Precedes Even
Square Follows Circle	Square Precedes Number	Circle Follows Even
	✓	

Question 12.		
Shapes Precede One-Digit Number	Shapes Precede Odd	Even Precedes Odd
Circle Precedes Even	Triangle Follows Square	Circle Precedes Rectangle
Number Follows Square	Square Precedes Triangle	Rectangle Precedes Even
Square Follows Circle	Odd Follows Shapes	Circle Follows Even
	✓	

Question 13.

Shapes Precede One-Digit Number	Shapes Precede Even	Even Precedes Odd
Even Follows Cross	Triangle Follows Cross	Circle Precedes Rectangle
Cross Follows Square	Circle Precedes Even	Rectangle Precedes Even
Square Follows Odd	Odd Precedes Shapes	Circle Precedes Even
✓		

Question 14.

Shapes Precede Two-Digit Number	Shapes Precede Even	Even Precedes Odd
Cross Precedes Triangle	Triangle Follows Square	Triangle Precedes Even One-Number Digit
Odd Follows Square	Square Precedes Triangle	Rectangle Precedes Even
Square Follows Cross	Shapes Follow Odd	Circle Follows Even
✓		

Question 15.

Square Precedes Circle	Shapes Precede Even	Even Precedes Odd
Cross Precedes Rectangle	Triangle Follows Square	Circle Follows Rectangle
Circle Follows Square	Square Precedes Triangle	Cross Follows Square
Square Precedes Cross	Two Digits Follow Single Digits	Square Precedes Circle
✓		

Rule Analysis – Test 2

You have 20 seconds to memorise the order of the list as per the direction of the arrows. Then turn over the page and identify the rules which match the order below.

Question 1.

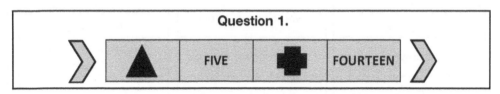

Question 2.

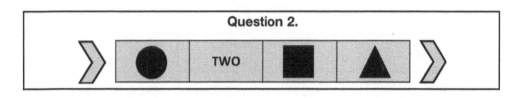

Question 3.

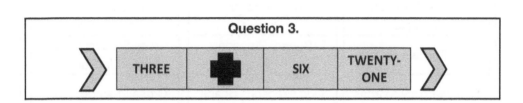

Question 1.		
Shapes Precede Two-Digit Number	Odd Precedes Even	Even Precedes Odd
Cross Precedes Triangle	Even Follows Cross	Circle Precedes Rectangle
Odd Follows Square	Cross Follows Triangle	Rectangle Precedes Even
Square Follows Cross	Odd Follows Triangle	Circle Follows Even

Question 2.		
Circle Precedes One-Digit Number	Shapes Precede Even	Even Precedes Odd
Square Follows Circle	Triangle Follows Square	Circle Precedes Rectangle
Even Follows Circle	Square Precedes Triangle	Rectangle Precedes Even
Square Precedes Triangle	Odd Precedes Shapes	Circle Follows Even

Question 3.		
Shape Precedes Two-Digit Number	Shape Precedes Even	Shape Precedes Two-Digit Number
Cross Precedes Triangle	Triangle Follows Square	Two-Digit Number Follows Even
Odd Follows Square	Square Precedes Triangle	Cross Follows Single-Digit Odd Number
Square Follows Cross	Odd Precedes Shape	Cross Precedes Even

Question 4.

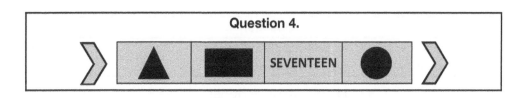

Question 5.

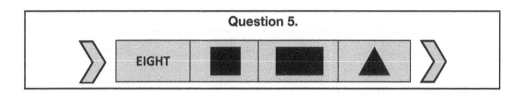

Question 6.

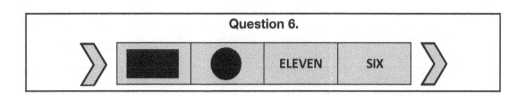

Question 4.

Shapes Precede Two-Digit Number	Rectangle Precedes Odd	Even Precedes Odd
Cross Precedes Triangle	Odd Follows Triangle	Circle Precedes Rectangle
Odd Follows Square	Circle Follows Triangle	Rectangle Precedes Even
Square Follows Cross	Rectangle Precedes Circle	Circle Follows Even
[ ]	[ ]	[ ]

Question 5.

Square Follows Even	Shapes Precede Even	Even Precedes Odd
Even Precedes Triangle	Triangle Follows Square	Circle Precedes Rectangle
Rectangle Follows Square	Square Precedes Triangle	Rectangle Precedes Even
Square Precedes Triangle	Odd Precedes Shapes	Circle Follows Even
[ ]	[ ]	[ ]

Question 6.

Shapes Precede Two-Digit Number	Shapes Precede Two-Digit Number	Even Follows Odd
Circle Precedes Rectangle	Even Precedes Odd	Circle Follows Rectangle
Numbers Follow Rectangle	Circle Precedes Rectangle	Rectangle Precedes Even
Even Follows Odd	Numbers Follow Rectangle	Circle Precedes Even
[ ]	[ ]	[ ]

Question 7.

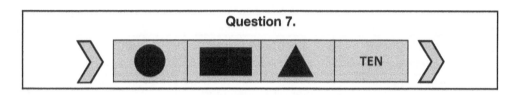

Question 8.

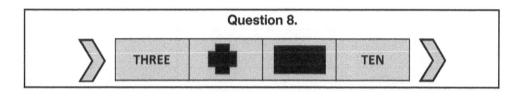

Question 9.

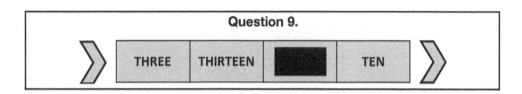

Question 7.

Shapes Precede Two-Digit Number	Shapes Precede Two-Digit Number	Number Follows Triangle
Circle Precedes Rectangle	Even Precedes Odd	Circle Precedes Rectangle
Number Follows Rectangle	Circle Precedes Rectangle	Rectangle Follows Circle
Even Follows Odd	Number Follows Rectangle	Even Follows Rectangle

Question 8.

Shapes Precede Two-Digit Number	Shapes Precede Two-Digit Number	Numbers Follow Triangle
Cross Precedes Rectangle	Even Precedes Odd	Circle Precedes Rectangle
Even Follows Rectangle	Circle Precedes Rectangle	Rectangle Follows Circle
Even Follows Odd	Numbers Follow Rectangle	Even Follows Rectangle

Question 9.

Shape Precedes Two-Digit Numbers	One Digit Precedes Two-Digit Numbers	Numbers Follow Triangle
Cross Precedes Rectangle	Odd Precedes Rectangle	Circle Precedes Rectangle
Even Follows Rectangle	Rectangle Precedes Even Two Digits	Rectangle Follows Circle
Even Follows Odd	Even Number Follows Rectangle	Even Follows Rectangle

Question 10.

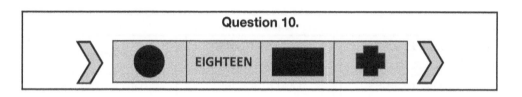

Question 11.

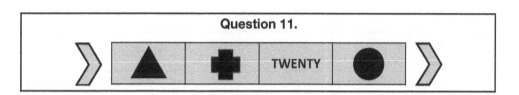

Question 12.

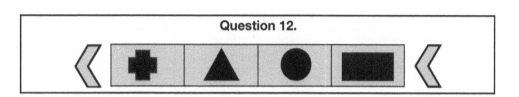

Question 10.

Shapes Precede Two-Digit Number	One-Digit Number Precedes Square	Number Follows Circle
Cross Precedes Rectangle	Odd Precedes Rectangle	Cross Follows Rectangle
Even Follows Rectangle	Rectangle Precedes Even Two Digits	Rectangle Follows Circle
Even Follows Odd	Even Number Follows Rectangle	Even Precedes Rectangle

Question 11.

Shapes Precede Two-Digit Number	Triangle Precedes Cross	Number Follows Circle
Cross Precedes Rectangle	Circle Follows Number	Cross Follows Rectangle
Even Follows Rectangle	Triangle Precedes Circle	Rectangle Follows Circle
Even Follows Odd	Even Number Follows Cross	Even Precedes Rectangle

Question 12.

Triangle Precedes Cross	Triangle Precedes Cross	Number Follows Circle
Circle Follows Rectangle	Circle Follows Number	Cross Follows Rectangle
Triangle Follows Rectangle	Triangle Precedes Circle	Rectangle Follows Circle
Cross Follows Rectangle	Even Number Follows Cross	Even Precedes Rectangle

Question 13.

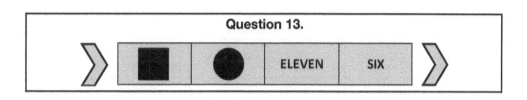

Question 14.

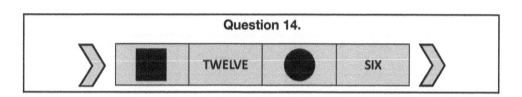

Question 15.

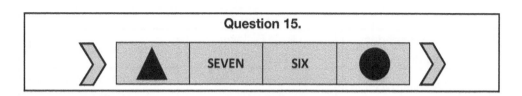

Question 13.

Even Precedes Odd	Even Precedes Odd	Even Follows Odd
Shapes Precede Numbers	Shapes Precede Numbers	Shapes Precede Numbers
Square Precedes Circle	Square Precedes Circle	Square Precedes Circle
Two Digits Follow Single Digits	Two Digits Follow Single Digits	Two Digits Precede Single Digits

Question 14.

Shapes Precede Numbers	Circle Follows Square	Two Digits Precede Single Digits
Square Precedes Circle	Odd Follows Even	Square Precedes Numbers
Two Digits Follow Single Digits	Two Digits Precede Single Digits	Even Follows Square
Even Precedes Odd	Square Follows Numbers	Circle Follows Two-Digit Number

Question 15.

Triangle Precedes Numbers	Circle Follows Numbers	Circle Follows Triangle
Circle Follows Triangle	Triangle Precedes Numbers	Triangle Follows Numbers
Numbers Precede Circle	Odd Precedes Even	Odd Precedes Even
Even Precedes Odd	Numbers Precede Circle	Numbers Precede Circle

ANSWERS OVERLEAF

Question 1.

Shapes Precede Two-Digit Number	Odd Precedes Even	Even Precedes Odd
Cross Precedes Triangle	Even Follows Cross	Circle Precedes Rectangle
Odd Follows Square	Cross Follows Triangle	Rectangle Precedes Even
Square Follows Cross	Odd Follows Triangle	Circle Follows Even
☐	✓	☐

Question 2.

Circle Precedes One-Digit Number	Shapes Precede Even	Even Precedes Odd
Square Follows Circle	Triangle Follows Square	Circle Precedes Rectangle
Even Follows Circle	Square Precedes Triangle	Rectangle Precedes Even
Square Precedes Triangle	Odd Precedes Shapes	Circle Follows Even
✓	☐	☐

Question 3.

Shape Precedes Two-Digit Number	Shape Precedes Even	Shape Precedes Two Digit Number
Cross Precedes Triangle	Triangle Follows Square	Two Digit Number Follows Even
Odd Follows Square	Square Precedes Triangle	Cross Follows Single Digit Odd Number
Square Follows Cross	Odd Precedes Shape	Cross Precedes Even
☐	☐	✓

Question 4.

Shapes Precede Two-Digit Number	Rectangle Precedes Odd	Even Precedes Odd
Cross Precedes Triangle	Odd Follows Triangle	Circle Precedes Rectangle
Odd Follows Square	Circle Follows Triangle	Rectangle Precedes Even
Square Follows Cross	Rectangle Precedes Circle	Circle Follows Even
	✓	

Question 5.

Square Follows Even	Shapes Precede Even	Even Precedes Odd
Even Precedes Triangle	Triangle Follows Square	Circle Precedes Rectangle
Rectangle Follows Square	Square Precedes Triangle	Rectangle Precedes Even
Square Precedes Triangle	Odd Precedes Shapes	Circle Follows Even
✓		

Question 6.

Shapes Precede Two-Digit Number	Shapes Precede Two-Digit Number	Even Follows Odd
Circle Precedes Rectangle	Even Precedes Odd	Circle Follows Rectangle
Numbers Follow Rectangle	Circle Precedes Rectangle	Rectangle Precedes Even
Even Follows Odd	Numbers Follow Rectangle	Circle Precedes Even
		✓

Question 7.

Shapes Precede Two-Digit Number	Shapes Precede Two-Digit Number	Number Follows Triangle
Circle Precedes Rectangle	Even Precedes Odd	Circle Precedes Rectangle
Number Follows Rectangle	Circle Precedes Rectangle	Rectangle Follows Circle
Even Follows Odd	Number Follows Rectangle	Even Follows Rectangle
☐	☐	☑

Question 8.

Shapes Precede Two-Digit Number	Shapes Precede Two-Digit Number	Numbers Follow Triangle
Cross Precedes Rectangle	Even Precedes Odd	Circle Precedes Rectangle
Even Follows Rectangle	Circle Precedes Rectangle	Rectangle Follows Circle
Even Follows Odd	Numbers Follow Rectangle	Even Follows Rectangle
☑	☐	☐

Question 9.

Shape Precedes Two-Digit Numbers	One Digit Precedes Two-Digit Numbers	Numbers Follow Triangle
Cross Precedes Rectangle	Odd Precedes Rectangle	Circle Precedes Rectangle
Even Follows Rectangle	Rectangle Precedes Even Two Digits	Rectangle Follows Circle
Even Follows Odd	Even Number Follows Rectangle	Even Follows Rectangle
☐	☑	☐

Question 10.

Shapes Precede Two-Digit Number	One-Digit Number Precedes Square	Number Follows Circle
Cross Precedes Rectangle	Odd Precedes Rectangle	Cross Follows Rectangle
Even Follows Rectangle	Rectangle Precedes Even Two Digits	Rectangle Follows Circle
Even Follows Odd	Even Number Follows Rectangle	Even Precedes Rectangle
☐	☐	✓

Question 11.

Shapes Precede Two-Digit Number	Triangle Precedes Cross	Number Follows Circle
Cross Precedes Rectangle	Circle Follows Number	Cross Follows Rectangle
Even Follows Rectangle	Triangle Precedes Circle	Rectangle Follows Circle
Even Follows Odd	Even Number Follows Cross	Even Precedes Rectangle
☐	✓	☐

Question 12.

Triangle Precedes Cross	Triangle Precedes Cross	Number Follows Circle
Circle Follows Rectangle	Circle Follows Number	Cross Follows Rectangle
Triangle Follows Rectangle	Triangle Precedes Circle	Rectangle Follows Circle
Cross Follows Rectangle	Even Number Follows Cross	Even Precedes Rectangle
✓	☐	☐

Question 13.

Even Precedes Odd	Even Precedes Odd	Even Follows Odd
Shapes Precede Numbers	Shapes Precede Numbers	Shapes Precede Numbers
Square Precedes Circle	Square Precedes Circle	Square Precedes Circle
Two Digits Follow Single Digits	Two Digits Follow Single Digits	Two Digits Precede Single Digits
☐	☐	✓

Question 14.

Shapes Precede Numbers	Circle Follows Square	Two Digits Precede Single Digits
Square Precedes Circle	Odd Follows Even	Square Precedes Numbers
Two Digits Follow Single Digits	Two Digits Precede Single Digits	Even Follows Square
Even Precedes Odd	Square Follows Numbers	Circle Follows Two-Digit Number
☐	☐	✓

Question 15.

Triangle Precedes Numbers	Circle Follows Numbers	Circle Follows Triangle
Circle Follows Triangle	Triangle Precedes Numbers	Triangle Follows Numbers
Numbers Precede Circle	Odd Precedes Even	Odd Precedes Even
Even Precedes Odd	Numbers Precede Circle	Numbers Precede Circle
☐	✓	☐

Rule Analysis – Test 3

You have 20 seconds to memorise the order of the list as per the direction of the arrows. Then turn over the page and identify the rules which match the order below.

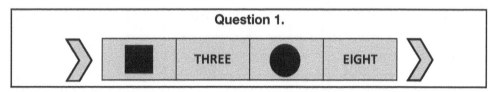

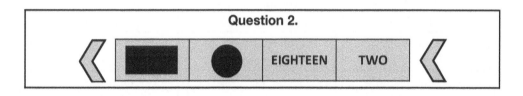

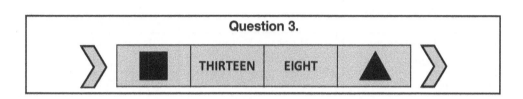

Question 1.

Circle Follows Square	Square Follows Numbers	Square Precedes Even
Even Follows Odd	Even Precedes Odd	Circle Precedes Square
Square Precedes Even	Numbers Follow Circle	Numbers Follow Square
Circle Precedes Even	Circle Precedes Square	Even Follows Odd

Question 2.

Numbers Precede Shapes	Rectangle Precedes Numbers	Numbers Precede Shapes
Rectangle Follows Circle	Two-Digit Number Precedes Circle	Circle Follows Rectangle
Rectangle Follows Numbers	Numbers Precede Shapes	Two-Digit Number Precedes Circle
Two-Digit Number Precedes Rectangle	Circle Follows Rectangle	Rectangle Follows Numbers

Question 3.

Triangle Follows Odd	Square Follows Numbers	Triangle Follows Odd
Even Follows Odd	Even Precedes Odd	Square Precedes Numbers
Numbers Follow Square	Numbers Follow Triangle	Numbers Follow Square
Square Follows Triangle	Triangle Follows Square	Triangle Follows Square

Question 4.

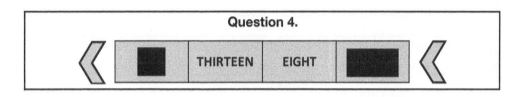

Question 5.

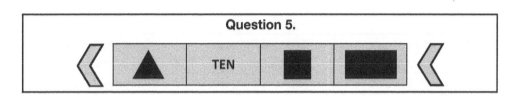

Question 6.

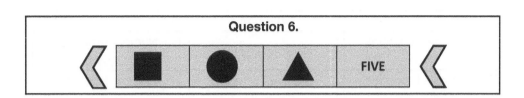

Question 4.

Rectangle Precedes Odd	Rectangle Precedes Odd	Square Precedes Numbers
Even Precedes Odd	Square Follows Numbers	Even Follows Odd
Numbers Precede Square	Numbers Precede Square	Numbers Precede Rectangle
Square Precedes Rectangle	Rectangle Precedes Square	Rectangle Precedes Square

Question 5.

Triangle Follows Number	Triangle Follows Number	Triangle Follows Number
Triangle Follows Square	Number Follows Square	Number Follows Square
Rectangle Precedes Square	Rectangle Precedes Triangle	Triangle Follows Square
Square Follows Triangle	Square Follows Triangle	Rectangle Precedes Square

Question 6.

Number Precedes Square	Circle Follows Number	Number Precedes Square
Triangle Precedes Square	Triangle Precedes Square	Triangle Precedes Circle
Circle Follows Number	Number Follows Circle	Circle Follows Square
Number Precedes Circle	Number Precedes Square	Number Precedes Circle

Question 7.

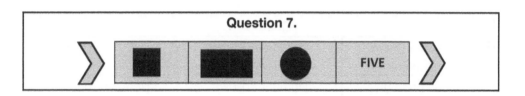

Question 8.

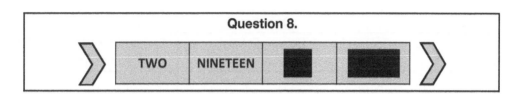

Question 9.

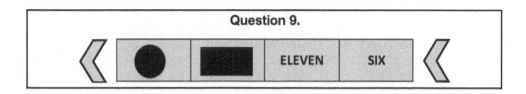

Question 7.

Number Follows Square	Rectangle Follows Square	Circle Precedes Square
Circle Precedes Number	Number Follows Square	Number Follows Square
Rectangle Follows Square	Circle Precedes Number	Rectangle Follows Circle
Number Precedes Circle	Number Follows Circle	Number Follows Circle
☐	☐	☐

Question 8.

Rectangle Follows Odd	Square Follows Numbers	Square Follows Numbers
Even Precedes Odd	Even Precedes Odd	Even Precedes Odd
Numbers Follow Square	Numbers Follow Rectangle	Shapes Follow Numbers
Square Follows Rectangle	Shapes Precede Numbers	Rectangle Follows Square
☐	☐	☐

Question 9.

Even Precedes Odd	Even Precedes Odd	Shapes Follow Two-Digit Number
Circle Follows Rectangle	Circle Follows Rectangle	Even Follows Odd
Rectangle Follows Odd	Circle Follows Odd	Circle Follows Rectangle
Rectangle Precedes Even	Rectangle Follows Even	Numbers Precede Rectangle
☐	☐	☐

Question 10.

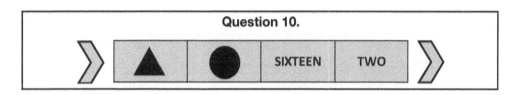

Question 11.

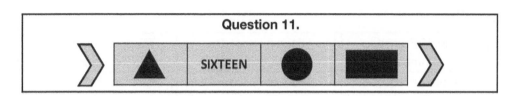

Question 12.

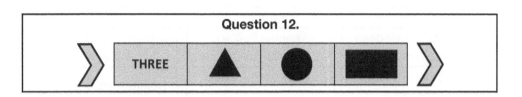

Question 10.

Triangle Follows Numbers	Numbers Follow Shapes	Numbers Follow Shapes
Two-Digit Number Follows Circle	Triangle Precedes Circle	Circle Precedes Triangle
Numbers Follow Shapes	Triangle Precedes Numbers	Two-Digit Number Follows Circle
Circle Precedes Triangle	Two-Digit Number Follows Triangle	Triangle Precedes Numbers

Question 11.

Triangle Precedes Number	Triangle Precedes Number	Triangle Precedes Number
Number Precedes Circle	Triangle Precedes Circle	Number Precedes Circle
Rectangle Follows Triangle	Rectangle Follows Circle	Triangle Precedes Circle
Circle Precedes Triangle	Circle Precedes Triangle	Rectangle Follows Circle

Question 12.

Number Precedes Circle	Triangle Follows Number	Number Precedes Circle
Triangle Follows Number	Triangle Precedes Circle	Triangle Follows Circle
Circle Precedes Triangle	Rectangle Follows Circle	Rectangle Follows Circle
Rectangle Follows Triangle	Circle Follows Number	Triangle Follows Number

Question 13.

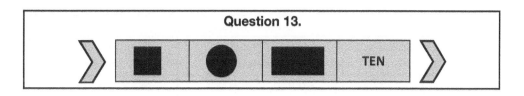

Question 14.

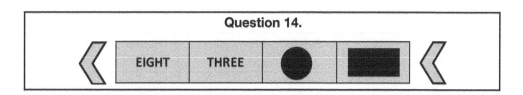

Question 15.

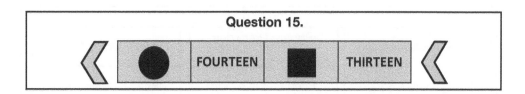

Question 13.

Number Follows Square	Circle Precedes Number	Number Follows Square
Rectangle Follows Square	Rectangle Follows Square	Rectangle Follows Circle
Circle Precedes Number	Number Precedes Circle	Circle Precedes Square
Number Follows Circle	Number Follows Square	Number Follows Circle

Question 14.

Circle Precedes Numbers	Rectangle Precedes Odd	Rectangle Precedes Numbers
Even Follows Odd	Even Follows Odd	Even Follows Odd
Numbers Precede Rectangle	Numbers Precede Circle	Shapes Precede Numbers
Shapes Follow Numbers	Square Precedes Rectangle	Rectangle Precedes Circle

Question 15.

Square Follows Even	Square Precedes Numbers	Circle Follows Square
Circle Follows Square	Even Follows Odd	Even Follows Odd
Numbers Precede Square	Circle Follows Even	Square Follows Odd
Even Precedes Odd	Circle Follows Square	Circle Follows Even

ANSWERS OVERLEAF

Question 1.

Circle Follows Square	Square Follows Numbers	Square Precedes Even
Even Follows Odd	Even Precedes Odd	Circle Precedes Square
Square Precedes Even	Numbers Follow Circle	Numbers Follow Square
Circle Precedes Even	Circle Precedes Square	Even Follows Odd
✓		

Question 2.

Numbers Precede Shapes	Rectangle Precedes Numbers	Numbers Precede Shapes
Rectangle Follows Circle	Two-Digit Number Precedes Circle	Circle Follows Rectangle
Rectangle Follows Numbers	Numbers Precede Shapes	Two-Digit Number Precedes Circle
Two-Digit Number Precedes Rectangle	Circle Follows Rectangle	Rectangle Follows Numbers
✓		

Question 3.

Triangle Follows Odd	Square Follows Numbers	Triangle Follows Odd
Even Follows Odd	Even Precedes Odd	Square Precedes Numbers
Numbers Follow Square	Numbers Follow Triangle	Numbers Follow Square
Square Follows Triangle	Triangle Follows Square	Triangle Follows Square
		✓

Question 4.

Rectangle Precedes Odd	Rectangle Precedes Odd	Square Precedes Numbers
Even Precedes Odd	Square Follows Numbers	Even Follows Odd
Numbers Precede Square	Numbers Precede Square	Numbers Precede Rectangle
Square Precedes Rectangle	Rectangle Precedes Square	Rectangle Precedes Square
	✓	

Question 5.

Triangle Follows Number	Triangle Follows Number	Triangle Follows Number
Triangle Follows Square	Number Follows Square	Number Follows Square
Rectangle Precedes Square	Rectangle Precedes Triangle	Triangle Follows Square
Square Follows Triangle	Square Follows Triangle	Rectangle Precedes Square
		✓

Question 6.

Number Precedes Square	Circle Follows Number	Number Precedes Square
Triangle Precedes Square	Triangle Precedes Square	Triangle Precedes Circle
Circle Follows Number	Number Follows Circle	Circle Follows Square
Number Precedes Circle	Number Precedes Square	Number Precedes Circle
✓		

Question 7.

Number Follows Square	Rectangle Follows Square	Circle Precedes Square
Circle Precedes Number	Number Follows Square	Number Follows Square
Rectangle Follows Square	Circle Precedes Number	Rectangle Follows Circle
Number Precedes Circle	Number Follows Circle	Number Follows Circle
☐	✓	☐

Question 8.

Rectangle Follows Odd	Square Follows Numbers	Square Follows Numbers
Even Precedes Odd	Even Precedes Odd	Even Precedes Odd
Numbers Follow Square	Numbers Follow Rectangle	Shapes Follow Numbers
Square Follows Rectangle	Shapes Precede Numbers	Rectangle Follows Square
☐	☐	✓

Question 9.

Even Precedes Odd	Even Precedes Odd	Shapes Follow Two-Digit Number
Circle Follows Rectangle	Circle Follows Rectangle	Even Follows Odd
Rectangle Follows Odd	Circle Follows Odd	Circle Follows Rectangle
Rectangle Precedes Even	Rectangle Follows Even	Numbers Precede Rectangle
☐	✓	☐

Question 10.

Triangle Follows Numbers	Numbers Follow Shapes	Numbers Follow Shapes
Two-Digit Number Follows Circle	Triangle Precedes Circle	Circle Precedes Triangle
Numbers Follow Shapes	Triangle Precedes Numbers	Two-Digit Number Follows Circle
Circle Precedes Triangle	Two-Digit Number Follows Triangle	Triangle Precedes Numbers
	✓	

Question 11.

Triangle Precedes Number	Triangle Precedes Number	Triangle Precedes Number
Number Precedes Circle	Triangle Precedes Circle	Number Precedes Circle
Rectangle Follows Triangle	Rectangle Follows Circle	Triangle Precedes Circle
Circle Precedes Triangle	Circle Precedes Triangle	Rectangle Follows Circle
		✓

Question 12.

Number Precedes Circle	Triangle Follows Number	Number Precedes Circle
Triangle Follows Number	Triangle Precedes Circle	Triangle Follows Circle
Circle Precedes Triangle	Rectangle Follows Circle	Rectangle Follows Circle
Rectangle Follows Triangle	Circle Follows Number	Triangle Follows Number
	✓	

Question 13.

Number Follows Square	Circle Precedes Number	Number Follows Square
Rectangle Follows Square	Rectangle Follows Square	Rectangle Follows Circle
Circle Precedes Number	Number Precedes Circle	Circle Precedes Square
Number Follows Circle	Number Follows Square	Number Follows Circle
✓		

Question 14.

Circle Precedes Numbers	Rectangle Precedes Odd	Rectangle Precedes Numbers
Even Follows Odd	Even Follows Odd	Even Follows Odd
Numbers Precede Rectangle	Numbers Precede Circle	Shapes Precede Numbers
Shapes Follow Numbers	Square Precedes Rectangle	Rectangle Precedes Circle
		✓

Question 15.

Square Follows Even	Square Precedes Numbers	Circle Follows Square
Circle Follows Square	Even Follows Odd	Even Follows Odd
Numbers Precede Square	Circle Follows Even	Square Follows Odd
Even Precedes Odd	Circle Follows Square	Circle Follows Even
		✓

Rule Analysis – Test 4

You have 20 seconds to memorise the order of the list as per the direction of the arrows. Then turn over the page and identify the rules which match the order below.

Question 1.

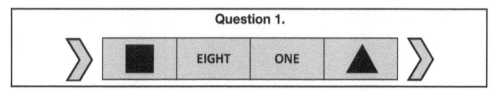

Question 2.

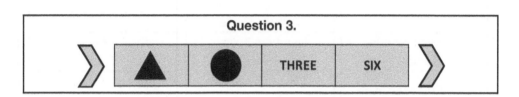

Question 3.

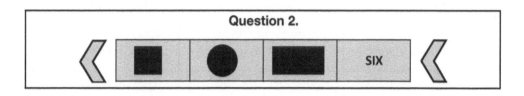

Question 1.

Square Follows Odd	Triangle Follows Odd	Square Follows Numbers
Even Follows Odd	Square Precedes Numbers	Even Precedes Odd
Numbers Precede Triangle	Numbers Follow Square	Numbers Follow Triangle
Square Follows Triangle	Triangle Follows Square	Triangle Follows Square

Question 2.

Number Precedes Square	Circle Follows Number	Number Precedes Square
Rectangle Precedes Square	Rectangle Precedes Square	Rectangle Precedes Circle
Circle Follows Number	Number Follows Circle	Circle Follows Square
Number Precedes Circle	Number Precedes Square	Number Precedes Circle

Question 3.

Circle Precedes Numbers	Triangle Follows Numbers	Numbers Follow Shapes
Triangle Precedes Circle	Two-Digit Number Follows Circle	Odd Precedes Even
Triangle Precedes Numbers	Numbers Follow Shapes	Circle Precedes Triangle
Odd Precedes Even	Circle Precedes Triangle	Triangle Precedes Numbers

Question 4.

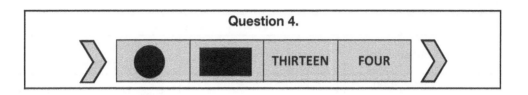

Question 5.

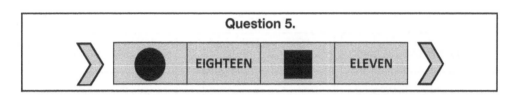

Question 6.

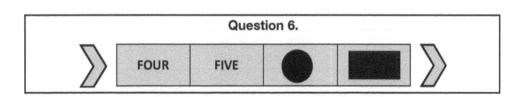

Question 4.

Even Follows Odd	Even Follows Odd	Shapes Precede Two-Digit Numbers
Circle Precedes Rectangle	Circle Precedes Rectangle	Even Precedes Odd
Rectangle Precedes Odd	Circle Precedes Odd	Circle Precedes Rectangle
Rectangle Follows Even	Rectangle Precedes Even	Numbers Follow Rectangle

Question 5.

Square Precedes Even	Square Follows Numbers	Circle Precedes Square
Circle Precedes Square	Even Precedes Odd	Even Precedes Odd
Numbers Follow Square	Circle Precedes Even	Square Precedes Odd
Even Follows Odd	Circle Precedes Square	Circle Precedes Even

Question 6.

Rectangle Follows Odd	Rectangle Follows Numbers	Circle Follows Numbers
Even Precedes Odd	Even Precedes Odd	Even Precedes Odd
Numbers Follow Circle	Shapes Follow Numbers	Numbers Follow Rectangle
Square Follows Rectangle	Rectangle Follows Circle	Shapes Precede Numbers

Question 7.

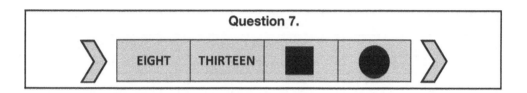

Question 8.

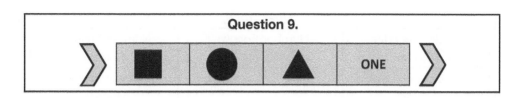

Question 9.

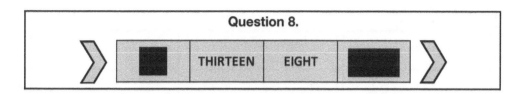

Question 7.

Circle Follows Odd	Square Follows Numbers	Square Follows Numbers
Even Precedes Odd	Even Precedes Odd	Even Precedes Odd
Numbers Follow Square	Numbers Follow Circle	Shapes Follow Numbers
Square Follows Circle	Shapes Precede Numbers	Circle Follows Square

Question 8.

Rectangle Follows Odd	Square Follows Numbers	Rectangle Follows Odd
Even Follows Odd	Even Precedes Odd	Square Precedes Numbers
Numbers Follow Square	Numbers Follow Rectangle	Numbers Follow Square
Square Follows Rectangle	Rectangle Follows Square	Rectangle Follows Square

Question 9.

Circle Precedes Number	Number Follows Square	Number Follows Square
Triangle Follows Square	Triangle Follows Circle	Triangle Follows Square
Number Precedes Circle	Circle Precedes Square	Circle Precedes Number
Number Follows Square	Number Follows Circle	Number Follows Circle

Question 10.

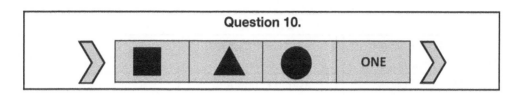

Question 11.

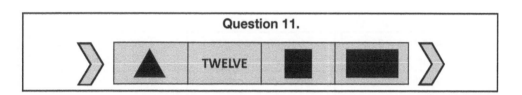

Question 12.

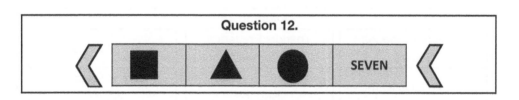

Question 10.

Triangle Follows Square	Number Follows Square	Circle Precedes Square
Number Follows Square	Circle Precedes Number	Number Follows Square
Circle Precedes Number	Triangle Follows Square	Triangle Follows Circle
Number Follows Circle	Number Precedes Circle	Number Follows Circle

☐	☐	☐

Question 11.

Triangle Precedes Number	Triangle Precedes Number	Triangle Precedes Number
Triangle Precedes Square	Number Precedes Square	Number Precedes Square
Rectangle Follows Square	Triangle Precedes Square	Rectangle Follows Triangle
Square Precedes Triangle	Rectangle Follows Square	Square Precedes Triangle

☐	☐	☐

Question 12.

Number Precedes Square	Triangle Precedes Square	Circle Follows Square
Circle Follows Number	Number Precedes Square	Number Precedes Square
Triangle Precedes Square	Circle Follows Number	Triangle Precedes Circle
Number Follows Circle	Number Precedes Circle	Number Precedes Circle

☐	☐	☐

Question 13.

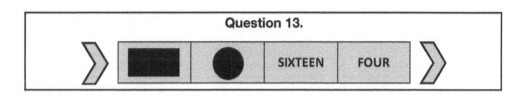

Question 14.

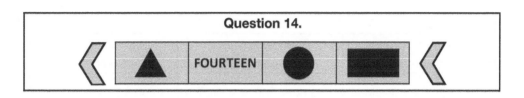

Question 15.

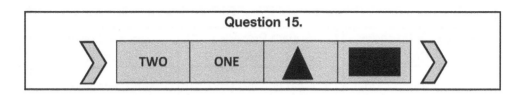

Question 13.

Rectangle Follows Numbers	Numbers Follow Shapes	Numbers Follow Shapes
Two-Digit Number Follows Circle	Circle Precedes Rectangle	Rectangle Precedes Circle
Numbers Follow Shapes	Two-Digit Number Follows Circle	Rectangle Precedes Numbers
Circle Precedes Rectangle	Rectangle Precedes Numbers	Two-Digit Number Follows Rectangle

Question 14.

Triangle Follows Number	Triangle Follows Number	Triangle Follows Number
Triangle Follows Circle	Number Follows Circle	Number Follows Circle
Rectangle Precedes Circle	Triangle Follows Circle	Rectangle Precedes Triangle
Circle Follows Triangle	Rectangle Precedes Circle	Circle Follows Triangle

Question 15.

Rectangle Precedes Odd	Square Precedes Numbers	Triangle Follows Numbers
Even Follows Odd	Even Follows Odd	Even Precedes Odd
Numbers Precede Circle	Shapes Precede Numbers	Numbers Precede Rectangle
Square Precedes Rectangle	Rectangle Precedes Circle	Shapes Follow Numbers

ANSWERS OVERLEAF

Question 1.

Square Follows Odd	Triangle Follows Odd	Square Follows Numbers
Even Follows Odd	Square Precedes Numbers	Even Precedes Odd
Numbers Precede Triangle	Numbers Follow Square	Numbers Follow Triangle
Square Follows Triangle	Triangle Follows Square	Triangle Follows Square
☐	✓	☐

Question 2.

Number Precedes Square	Circle Follows Number	Number Precedes Square
Rectangle Precedes Square	Rectangle Precedes Square	Rectangle Precedes Circle
Circle Follows Number	Number Follows Circle	Circle Follows Square
Number Precedes Circle	Number Precedes Square	Number Precedes Circle
✓	☐	☐

Question 3.

Circle Precedes Numbers	Triangle Follows Numbers	Numbers Follow Shapes
Triangle Precedes Circle	Two-Digit Number Follows Circle	Odd Precedes Even
Triangle Precedes Numbers	Numbers Follow Shapes	Circle Precedes Triangle
Odd Precedes Even	Circle Precedes Triangle	Triangle Precedes Numbers
✓	☐	☐

Question 4.

Even Follows Odd	Even Follows Odd	Shapes Precede Two-Digit Numbers
Circle Precedes Rectangle	Circle Precedes Rectangle	Even Precedes Odd
Rectangle Precedes Odd	Circle Precedes Odd	Circle Precedes Rectangle
Rectangle Follows Even	Rectangle Precedes Even	Numbers Follow Rectangle
	✓	

Question 5.

Square Precedes Even	Square Follows Numbers	Circle Precedes Square
Circle Precedes Square	Even Precedes Odd	Even Precedes Odd
Numbers Follow Square	Circle Precedes Even	Square Precedes Odd
Even Follows Odd	Circle Precedes Square	Circle Precedes Even
		✓

Question 6.

Rectangle Follows Odd	Rectangle Follows Numbers	Circle Follows Numbers
Even Precedes Odd	Even Precedes Odd	Even Precedes Odd
Numbers Follow Circle	Shapes Follow Numbers	Numbers Follow Rectangle
Square Follows Rectangle	Rectangle Follows Circle	Shapes Precede Numbers
	✓	

Question 7.

Circle Follows Odd	Square Follows Numbers	Square Follows Numbers
Even Precedes Odd	Even Precedes Odd	Even Precedes Odd
Numbers Follow Square	Numbers Follow Circle	Shapes Follow Numbers
Square Follows Circle	Shapes Precede Numbers	Circle Follows Square
		✓

Question 8.

Rectangle Follows Odd	Square Follows Numbers	Rectangle Follows Odd
Even Follows Odd	Even Precedes Odd	Square Precedes Numbers
Numbers Follow Square	Numbers Follow Rectangle	Numbers Follow Square
Square Follows Rectangle	Rectangle Follows Square	Rectangle Follows Square
		✓

Question 9.

Circle Precedes Number	Number Follows Square	Number Follows Square
Triangle Follows Square	Triangle Follows Circle	Triangle Follows Square
Number Precedes Circle	Circle Precedes Square	Circle Precedes Number
Number Follows Square	Number Follows Circle	Number Follows Circle
		✓

Question 10.

Triangle Follows Square	Number Follows Square	Circle Precedes Square
Number Follows Square	Circle Precedes Number	Number Follows Square
Circle Precedes Number	Triangle Follows Square	Triangle Follows Circle
Number Follows Circle	Number Precedes Circle	Number Follows Circle
✓		

Question 11.

Triangle Precedes Number	Triangle Precedes Number	Triangle Precedes Number
Triangle Precedes Square	Number Precedes Square	Number Precedes Square
Rectangle Follows Square	Triangle Precedes Square	Rectangle Follows Triangle
Square Precedes Triangle	Rectangle Follows Square	Square Precedes Triangle
	✓	

Question 12.

Number Precedes Square	Triangle Precedes Square	Circle Follows Square
Circle Follows Number	Number Precedes Square	Number Precedes Square
Triangle Precedes Square	Circle Follows Number	Triangle Precedes Circle
Number Follows Circle	Number Precedes Circle	Number Precedes Circle
	✓	

Question 13.

Rectangle Follows Numbers	Numbers Follow Shapes	Numbers Follow Shapes
Two-Digit Number Follows Circle	Circle Precedes Rectangle	Rectangle Precedes Circle
Numbers Follow Shapes	Two-Digit Number Follows Circle	Rectangle Precedes Numbers
Circle Precedes Rectangle	Rectangle Precedes Numbers	Two-Digit Number Follows Rectangle
		✓

Question 14.

Triangle Follows Number	Triangle Follows Number	Triangle Follows Number
Triangle Follows Circle	Number Follows Circle	Number Follows Circle
Rectangle Precedes Circle	Triangle Follows Circle	Rectangle Precedes Triangle
Circle Follows Triangle	Rectangle Precedes Circle	Circle Follows Triangle
	✓	

Question 15.

Rectangle Precedes Odd	Square Precedes Numbers	Triangle Follows Numbers
Even Follows Odd	Even Follows Odd	Even Precedes Odd
Numbers Precede Circle	Shapes Precede Numbers	Numbers Precede Rectangle
Square Precedes Rectangle	Rectangle Precedes Circle	Shapes Follow Numbers
		✓

A Few Final Words

Congratulations! You've made it to the end of this workbook. You should now be more confident than ever with regards to the Army Aptitude Tests. Additionally, you're in a great position to continue practising for the range of questions that you might face in the Army Aptitude Tests.

Here are some final tips before you go:

When answering Spatial Reasoning questions, pay close attention to whether or not you need to rotate clockwise or anti-clockwise. Careless candidates will only read the number of degrees to rotate by, and not the direction to rotate in! Also, try working in chunks. 45 degrees is half a chunk, 90 degrees is 1 chunk, 180 degrees is 2 chunks, and so on. Use this to help you visualise how many chunks you need to rotate the shape by.

Rule Analysis can be extremely tricky, but remember to work through one column at a time. As soon as you find a rule that does not follow the order of shapes and numbers, rule the entire column out and move onto the next one. Repeat this process until you find your answer. If you have the time, check all three columns: there will always be one correct column and two incorrect columns.

In addition, pay attention to the chevrons on either side of the order of shapes and numbers. These will reverse the order, and therefore completely change the correct answer!

The majority of candidates who pass the British Army selection process have a number of common factors. These are as follows:

1. They believe in themselves.

The first factor is self-belief. Regardless of what anyone tells you, you can pass the selection process and you can achieve high scores. Just like any job of this nature, you have to be prepared to work hard in order to be successful. You will notice that the Army Aptitude Tests are tough. Make sure you have the self-belief to pass the selection process and fill your mind with positive thoughts.

2. They prepare fully.

The second factor is preparation. Those people who achieve in life prepare fully for every eventuality and that is what you must do when you apply to join the Army and sit the Army Aptitude Tests. Work very hard and especially concentrate on your weak areas. By comparing your answers to ours, identify the areas that you are weak on and go all out to improve them.

3. They persevere.

Perseverance is a fantastic word. Everybody comes across obstacles or setbacks in their life, but it is what you do about those setbacks that is important. If you fail at something, then ask yourself 'why' have I failed? This will allow you to improve for next time and if you keep improving and trying, success will eventually follow. Apply this same method of thinking when you apply to join the Army.

4. They are self-motivated.

How much do you want to join the Army? Do you want it, or do you really want it? When you apply to join the Army, you should want it more than anything in the world. Your levels of self-motivation will shine through when you walk into the AFCO and when you attend the interview. For the weeks and months leading up to the selection process, be motivated as best you can, and always keep your fitness levels up, as this will serve to increase your levels of motivation.

Work hard, stay focused, and secure your dream career...

The how2become team

The How2Become Team.

IMPROVE YOUR ARMED FORCES SCORES!

Our How2Become Armed Forces guides are the ULTIMATE revision resources to prepare you fully for joining the Army.

FOR MORE INFORMATION ON OUR ARMY GUIDES, PLEASE CHECK OUT THE FOLLOWING:

WWW.HOW2BECOME.COM